Socrates and the Boy Who Asked Why

Leo Storm

Copyright © 2025 Leo Storm

All rights reserved.

ISBN: 9798312742329

CONTENTS

1. The Curious Boy — 1
2. Lessons in the Agora — 11
3. Fearing the Truth — 19
4. The Trial Begins — 28
5. A Test of Courage — 36
6. Legacy of Questions — 45

1 THE CURIOUS BOY

The sun shone brightly over Athens, casting warm golden light on the lively Agora. Merchants called out to passing citizens, selling olives, fish, and brightly woven fabrics. The smell of fresh bread and roasted lamb drifted through the air, mingling with the salty breeze from the sea. Philosophers gathered in groups, their voices rising and falling in spirited debate. In the midst of it all was Alex, an eleven-year-old boy with bright green eyes that sparkled with curiosity.

"Why does the sun rise in the east and not the west?" Alex asked, his voice filled with wonder.

His friend Demos groaned. "Not again, Alex. Why do you always have to ask so many questions?"

"Because I want to understand," Alex said simply. "Don't you ever wonder why things are the way they are?"

Demos shrugged. "Not really. Some things just are. Why do you care so much?"

Alex frowned. That answer never satisfied him. He turned to a group of boys playing with wooden dice. "What makes something fair? If you win the game, but the dice were carved unevenly, is it still fair?"

One of the boys, Lykos, rolled his eyes. "It's just a game, Alex. Stop thinking so much!"

Frustrated, Alex kicked a loose pebble on the ground. He didn't understand why no one else wanted to ask questions. The world was full of mysteries, and he wanted to uncover them all.

Unbeknownst to Alex, an old man with a scruffy white beard and twinkling eyes had been watching him from a distance. He sat on a low stone bench, his robe slightly worn and his sandals dusty from walking through the city. A smile played at his lips as he observed the boy's relentless curiosity.

The old man chuckled softly. "You ask very interesting questions, young one."

Alex turned to the voice and found himself looking at a man he had seen before but never spoken to—Socrates, the strange philosopher who spent his days talking to people in the Agora.

Alex hesitated. "You think so?"

"Oh, certainly," Socrates said, standing up. His voice was warm, his expression inviting. "You see, asking questions is how we discover the truth. But tell me, Alex, do you believe you already know the answers?"

Alex blinked. "Well… no. That's why I ask."

"Ah!" Socrates raised a finger. "That is wisdom already. To know that you do not know—that is the beginning of true knowledge."

Alex thought about this. "But how do I find the answers?"

Socrates chuckled. "By asking better questions."

Demos, who had been listening from a few steps away, folded his arms. "That doesn't make sense. How can you find answers by asking more questions?"

Socrates turned to him. "Let me ask you this, my young friend. What makes a good friend?"

Demos blinked. "Um… someone who stands by you and helps you when you need them."

Socrates nodded. "Very well. But is a friend still a good friend if he only helps you when it benefits him?"

Demos frowned. "No… that wouldn't be real friendship."

Socrates smiled. "Ah, you see? You started with one idea, but by asking a question, we found a deeper truth. This is how we learn—not by accepting, but by questioning."

Alex's heart pounded with excitement. He had never met an adult who encouraged his questions before. He had so many more to ask.

But before he could speak, a stern voice interrupted.

"Enough of this nonsense!"

Alex turned to see Councilman Antiphon, a tall, imposing man dressed in fine robes. He frowned at

Socrates. "Must you fill the boy's head with dangerous ideas? Athens has no need for idle thinkers."

Socrates bowed slightly, unfazed. "And yet, my dear Antiphon, Athens has always thrived on thought and discussion. Why silence what has built our great city?"

Antiphon's eyes narrowed. "Because some thoughts are dangerous."

Alex looked between them, confused. Why would questions be dangerous? They were just words—just thoughts. But as he watched Antiphon's cold expression, a strange feeling settled in his stomach. He had a sense that asking questions might not always be welcome.

Socrates simply smiled and turned back to Alex. "Keep asking, my boy. The pursuit of truth is the greatest adventure of all."

Antiphon scoffed and strode away. Demos shot Alex a nervous glance. "Maybe you should stop talking to him, Alex. You don't want to get in trouble."

But Alex wasn't so sure. He had a feeling that he had just met the most interesting man in Athens.

Later that afternoon, Alex walked beside Socrates through the busy streets of Athens. He had a hundred questions racing through his mind.

"Why do people get angry when I ask questions?" he finally asked.

Socrates chuckled. "Ah, an excellent question! Tell me, Alex, have you ever seen a man who believes he is very wise?"

Alex nodded. "Yes. The councilmen and some of the teachers."

"Indeed. And do they like being told they might be wrong?"

"No… they get upset," Alex admitted.

Socrates smiled. "Exactly. Many people do not seek the truth—they seek to be right. And when questions challenge their beliefs, they feel threatened."

Alex thought about this. "But if they're wrong, wouldn't they want to know?"

"One would hope so," Socrates said with a wink. "But not everyone values truth more than comfort."

Alex was quiet for a moment. He thought of his friends in the Agora, of Demos, and even of Councilman Antiphon. Did they fear questions? Was that why they pushed them away?

Socrates patted his shoulder. "You are on a journey, my young friend. But remember, questions alone are not enough. You must also seek wisdom, not just answers."

Alex frowned. "How do I do that?"

Socrates grinned. "By questioning not only the world—but also yourself."

That evening, as the sun dipped below the hills, Alex sat with his mother Myra outside their small home. The scent of olive oil and warm bread filled the air.

"You look thoughtful," Myra said, setting a bowl of fresh figs in front of him.

Alex sighed. "Mother, do you think it's bad to ask too many questions?"

She tilted her head. "Why do you ask?"

Alex hesitated. "Because it makes people uncomfortable. Demos gets annoyed. The councilmen don't like it. Even some of the teachers get frustrated."

Myra smiled softly and brushed a curl from his forehead. "Questions are not bad, Alex. They are how we learn. But sometimes, people fear what they do not understand."

Alex looked down at his hands. "Socrates says I should always keep questioning."

She nodded. "He is a wise man. But you must also learn when to listen, and when to be careful. The world is not always kind to those who think differently."

Alex chewed on her words. He wasn't sure he understood completely. But he did know one thing—he wasn't going to stop asking questions.

Not now. Not ever.

2 LESSONS IN THE AGORA

The sun sat high in the sky, casting golden light over the Agora, the heart of Athens. The square bustled with activity—merchants hawked their goods, bakers set out fresh loaves, and children wove through the crowd, playing games. But amidst the clamor of daily life, a different kind of gathering was forming near a stone fountain.

Here, Socrates stood in his usual spot, his robe slightly tattered, his eyes bright with anticipation. A few townspeople had already begun to gather, curious about what today's discussion might bring. And at his side, with a mixture of excitement and nervousness, stood Alex.

"Today, my friends," Socrates called, his voice carrying over the noise of the marketplace, "I wish to ask a simple question. What is truth?"

A murmur spread through the crowd. Some crossed their arms, skeptical. Others tilted their heads, considering. Thales, a thoughtful townsman, stroked his beard.

"What kind of question is that?" grumbled an older man. "Truth is truth. What else could it be?"

Socrates smiled. "Ah, but if truth is so simple, then why do so many people disagree about it?"

Alex's heart pounded. He knew the answer to this one! Raising his hand eagerly, he called out, "Maybe people see things differently because they have different experiences?"

Socrates clapped his hands. "Ah! An excellent thought, young Alex. So, tell me—if two men see the same event but tell different stories about it, which one is true?"

Alex hesitated. "I guess… maybe both? Or neither?"

The crowd chuckled at his uncertainty, but Socrates nodded approvingly. "Very good. The moment we begin to question what we know, we are already closer to understanding."

Alex beamed, thrilled to be a part of the discussion. The air in the Agora felt alive with possibility.

But then, a familiar voice cut through the moment.

"That's ridiculous," scoffed Demos, stepping forward from the crowd. His arms were folded, and his brow furrowed in irritation. "If you keep questioning everything, you'll never know anything at all."

The laughter from the crowd grew louder, this time not at Socrates, but at Alex. A flicker of doubt crept into his chest.

Socrates, however, remained unshaken. "Ah, Demos, an interesting point! Tell me, do you believe the things your father tells you?"

Demos frowned. "Of course."

"And your teachers?"

"Yes," Demos replied, though with less certainty.

Socrates nodded. "And what if one day they tell you something that you know is wrong? Will you still believe it just because they say so?"

Demos hesitated. The crowd quieted.

"I… I don't know," Demos muttered, shifting his weight uncomfortably.

Socrates chuckled. "Then you see, my young friend, questioning does not make us ignorant. It helps us decide for ourselves what is worth believing."

Some of the townsfolk murmured in agreement, but Demos only scowled. "Or maybe it just makes people confused."

With that, he turned and stalked off.

Alex watched his friend disappear into the crowd, a sinking feeling in his chest.

For the first time, he wasn't sure if asking questions made him wise… or just foolish.

The lively energy of the Agora faded as Alex followed Socrates toward a quieter part of the square. Here, under the shade of an old olive tree, the sounds of the marketplace softened, leaving only the occasional chatter of birds and the distant hum of the city.

Alex sat down on a smooth rock, staring at the dust beneath his sandals. He had felt so proud during the discussion—but now, Demos' words gnawed at him.

Socrates sat beside him, stretching his legs out lazily. "Ah, silence. A fine companion for thought, don't you agree?"

Alex nodded absently.

Socrates glanced at him, his eyes twinkling. "Tell me, my boy, what troubles you?"

Alex hesitated before blurting out, "What if Demos is right? What if I'm just making everything more confusing?"

Socrates chuckled. "Ah, confusion! A most valuable teacher."

Alex frowned. "But confusion feels… bad."

Socrates leaned back against the tree. "Yes, it can. But tell me, Alex—have you ever climbed a steep hill?"

Alex nodded. "Yes."

"And was it easy?"

"No, it was hard."

Socrates smiled. "Yet, when you reached the top, could you see farther than before?"

Alex blinked. He hadn't thought of it that way.

"The mind is much the same," Socrates continued. "When we question, we struggle. We doubt. But that is how we grow. Those who never climb never see beyond the valley they are in."

Alex sat with that thought for a long moment. "So… doubt isn't a bad thing?"

Socrates shook his head. "No, my boy. Doubt is the first step toward wisdom."

A warm breeze rustled the leaves above them. Alex felt a strange mixture of relief and determination settle in his chest.

Maybe he didn't have all the answers yet.

But that just meant he had more questions to ask.

And he couldn't wait to ask them.

3 FEARING THE TRUTH

The Agora was quieter than usual as the sun dipped toward the horizon, painting the stone buildings of Athens in hues of amber and gold. Vendors were beginning to pack up their goods, but a small group remained clustered near the old stone fountain, their voices low yet eager.

At the center of the gathering stood Socrates, his worn robe flowing gently in the evening breeze. He spoke with his usual warmth and conviction, his hands gesturing as he invited those around him to think beyond what they had always been told.

"What is justice?" he asked the townspeople. "Is it simply following the laws, or is it something greater?"

A few murmurs rippled through the crowd.

A potter named Lysias spoke up. "Justice is what keeps the city strong. Without laws, there would be chaos."

Socrates nodded thoughtfully. "Ah, but tell me—if a law is unjust, should it still be followed?"

A hush fell over the listeners. Some shifted uncomfortably.

Standing at the edge of the gathering, Thales watched intently, admiration and worry battling within him. He had always respected Socrates. The man was different from the other thinkers in Athens—he asked questions that made people see the world in a new light. And yet…

"This is dangerous," Thales muttered to his friend, Nicos, who stood beside him.

Nicos glanced at him. "You admire him, don't you?"

Thales hesitated. "I do. But I fear for him."

At that moment, he overheard a pair of men nearby whispering. Their voices were low but edged with unease.

"Socrates makes people question things best left unquestioned," one of them muttered.

"If he keeps this up, he'll make enemies of the wrong people," the other added.

Thales' stomach twisted. The city had always valued debate, but this felt different. There was a tension in Athens, a growing fear of those who dared to challenge tradition.

He clenched his fists. He didn't want to see harm come to Socrates. But how could one man protect another from the invisible force of fear?

As the sun dipped below the rooftops, Thales made a silent vow. He would do what he could to help Socrates—but he would have to be careful.

The following afternoon, the main square of Athens was packed. Citizens gathered in a semicircle, murmuring in curiosity and anticipation. At the center of it all, standing on the steps of the council hall, was Councilman Antiphon.

His deep voice carried over the crowd.

"My fellow Athenians," he began, his tone measured but firm. "We are a great city, built on the wisdom of our ancestors and the strength of our laws. And yet, there are those who wish to undermine these very foundations."

A murmur spread through the crowd.

Antiphon continued. "A man walks among us, spreading ideas that challenge our traditions, that make our children question their elders, that disrupt the harmony we have built. I ask you—can a city survive if its people no longer respect its values?"

A chorus of agreement rose from some in the crowd. Others exchanged uncertain glances.

A young man spoke up. "But Socrates only asks questions! Is that truly dangerous?"

Antiphon's eyes narrowed slightly. "Ah, my young friend, and what happens when too many questions are asked? When doubt takes root, chaos follows. Athenian unity is built on trust in our leaders, in our gods, in the wisdom passed down through generations. If we let men like Socrates turn questioning into a virtue, soon, there will be nothing left to hold us together."

Some cheered, others shifted uncomfortably.

Thales stood in the crowd, his jaw clenched. Socrates was no traitor. But Antiphon knew how to stir fear.

As the councilman raised his hands, his voice deepened. "I warn you, citizens of Athens—if we do not put an end to this dangerous talk, we may soon find our city crumbling from within."

The cheers grew louder, but not everyone joined in.

Among those who remained silent was Alex, standing near the back, his small hands curled into fists.

Later that day, in the schoolyard, Alex sat on a low stone bench, staring at the dust beneath his sandals. Around him, his friends played, laughing and shouting as they tossed a ball back and forth.

But Alex wasn't playing.

Demos plopped down beside him. "Still thinking about your philosopher friend?"

Alex didn't answer.

Lykos, one of the older boys, snorted. "You should stop hanging around Socrates. Haven't you heard? The council's watching him. People say he's dangerous."

Alex looked up. "Dangerous? He just asks questions."

"That's the problem," Demos muttered. "People don't like questions."

Alex frowned. "But aren't questions how we learn?"

Lykos scoffed. "Listen, Alex. If you keep following him around, people will start thinking you're just as foolish as he is."

Alex felt a wave of doubt crash over him. Hadn't he already felt the weight of people's judgment? Even at home, his mother had warned him to be careful.

And yet…

He thought of Socrates under the olive tree, telling him that doubt was the first step toward wisdom. He thought of how his own questions had led him to understand things he had never considered before.

Was he really willing to give that up just because others disapproved?

Taking a deep breath, he stood up.

"Maybe," he said carefully, "it's not Socrates who's foolish. Maybe it's the people who are too afraid to think."

The schoolyard fell silent.

Demos stared at him. Lykos let out a dry laugh. "Suit yourself, Alex. Just don't come crying when you get yourself into trouble."

Alex watched them walk away, his heart pounding.

For the first time, he felt truly alone.

But at the same time—deep inside—he felt stronger than ever.

4 THE TRIAL BEGINS

The courthouse loomed over the Athenian square, its weathered stone walls standing tall against the restless murmurs of the gathered crowd. Citizens of all kinds—merchants, scholars, farmers, and young boys like Alex—had come to witness the trial of Socrates.

The air crackled with tension. Some whispered with concern, others with anticipation. A few men, their faces set in hard lines, wore the insignia of the council—supporters of the prosecution.

Alex's stomach twisted. He shouldn't be here. His mother had warned him to stay away. But how could he? Socrates was his mentor, his friend.

He squeezed through the crowd until he spotted Demos, standing with a group of boys near the edge of the square. Alex waved, relieved to see his friend.

Demos, however, barely acknowledged him. His arms were crossed, his gaze locked on the raised platform where the trial was about to begin.

Alex's chest tightened. Something felt different.

Suddenly, Councilman Antiphon stepped forward. His robes were pristine, his posture rigid with authority. With a slow, deliberate motion, he raised his hand, signaling silence.

"All of Athens has gathered here today," he began, his voice strong and unwavering. "We stand in defense of our city, our traditions, and the minds of our youth."

Alex felt his pulse quicken.

"This man, Socrates, has been accused of corrupting the young and disrespecting the gods. He sows doubt where there should be certainty. He tears at the fabric of our great city with endless questions and reckless challenges to our way of life."

A murmur of agreement rippled through the crowd.

Alex's breath caught. How could they say that? Socrates didn't corrupt anyone—he made people think.

Then, amidst the crowd, a familiar, calm voice rose.

"I have merely asked what is just, Councilman," Socrates said, stepping forward. His simple robes were no match for the grandeur of his accusers, but his presence filled the space nonetheless. "If asking questions is a crime, then is the truth also guilty?"

The crowd stirred—some scoffed, others exchanged uneasy glances.

Alex clenched his fists. He knew Socrates was right. But as he glanced at Demos, his friend's face was unreadable.

And suddenly, Alex wondered: what if Demos thought Socrates was guilty?

When the trial paused for a short recess, Alex pushed through the crowd, hurrying to find Demos.

"Demos! Did you hear that?" Alex said breathlessly. "Socrates is only asking questions! How can they call that corruption?"

Demos turned to him, his expression unreadable. Then, after a moment, he spoke. "Maybe they're right, Alex."

Alex felt like the ground had dropped beneath him.

"What?"

Demos sighed, rubbing his forehead. "Look, I know you admire Socrates, but… maybe he's gone too far. Maybe questioning everything just makes people uncertain. Maybe that's dangerous."

Alex shook his head. "How can thinking be dangerous? What if we just accept everything without question? Then we're no better than—than sheep!"

Demos' eyes flashed with frustration. "And what if questioning everything means we lose what we have? Athens has lasted this long because of our laws, our beliefs! What if Socrates makes people stop trusting them?"

Alex's heart pounded. "Demos, that's what he's trying to teach us! To question means to understand, not destroy!"

But Demos stepped back, his expression guarded.

"I don't know, Alex," he said, his voice quieter now. "All I know is that my father thinks Socrates is a threat. And a lot of other people do too."

Alex opened his mouth, but before he could respond, a new chant rose from the crowd—low at first, then louder.

"Socrates must go! Socrates must go!"

Demos turned and, without looking back, joined the voices.

Alex felt his stomach drop.

He had never felt more alone.

As the sun dipped below the rooftops of Athens, the trial's first session came to an end. The crowd began to disperse, voices buzzing with discussion, some triumphant, others uncertain.

Alex found a quiet bench near the courthouse, where the shadows stretched long against the stone walls. His thoughts churned.

Demos had always been his friend. They had played together, laughed together. But today, it felt like a wall had risen between them—a wall built from fear and doubt.

He exhaled slowly, his mind drifting to Socrates' words under the olive tree.

"Doubt is the first step toward wisdom."

Was this what Socrates had meant? That seeking truth meant sometimes standing alone?

Nearby, a small group of citizens continued arguing over the trial.

"Socrates is a danger," one said. "He makes people question too much."

"But isn't that how we grow?" another challenged. "Why should we fear ideas?"

Alex listened, feeling a flicker of hope. Not everyone wanted Socrates silenced. There were others who believed in what was right.

Maybe he wasn't alone after all.

Taking a deep breath, Alex straightened his back. Tomorrow, the trial would continue. And so would he.

Because some things were worth standing up for—even if it meant standing alone.

5 A TEST OF COURAGE

The courthouse was more crowded than ever, a sea of faces packed tightly together. The air was thick with murmurs, whispers floating between the spectators like an uneasy wind. Some leaned forward eagerly, waiting for the moment Socrates would finally be silenced. Others, brows furrowed, seemed unsure—caught between admiration and fear.

At the heart of it all stood Socrates.

He was neither shaken nor afraid. His hands were clasped behind his back, his robe simple, his posture relaxed. His eyes scanned the crowd, pausing for just a moment—on Alex.

Alex felt his stomach twist into knots. He hadn't meant to catch Socrates' gaze. He had only wanted to be here, to see, to understand. But now... now he felt like he was being asked something without words.

A silent question.

What do you stand for?

He swallowed hard.

"Silence!" The sharp voice of the magistrate rang through the air, and the murmuring ceased.

Councilman Antiphon took his place before the jury, his expression unreadable. But his voice carried the weight of authority.

"We are gathered today to determine the fate of Socrates of Athens—a man accused of corrupting the youth and dishonoring the gods."

Alex's chest tightened. The words felt unreal, absurd. How could seeking the truth be a crime?

Socrates did not flinch. He did not protest. He simply waited.

Antiphon's voice rose. "The accused has spread dangerous ideas, questioning the laws that govern us, the traditions that hold our city together. What happens when a man teaches children to doubt their elders? To challenge authority? Is that wisdom?"

A few scattered shouts of agreement echoed from the back of the courtroom.

Antiphon turned sharply toward Socrates. "What do you say for yourself?"

A hush fell over the courthouse.

Socrates stepped forward.

And then, with steady calm, he spoke.

"Men of Athens," Socrates began, his voice even, unshaken. "I am accused of corrupting the youth. And yet, I have done nothing but ask questions."

His words cut through the silence, strong yet without anger.

"Tell me—should a man be punished for asking if something is just? Should he be condemned for searching for truth?"

Alex's breath caught. He could see the faces of the jury, some leaning in, listening despite themselves.

Socrates continued.

"I do not claim to be wise. In fact, I know that I know nothing—and that is what makes me different. Others believe they hold the truth without question. I simply ask if that truth is real."

A murmur rippled through the crowd.

Alex saw Demos near the front, his arms folded tightly across his chest, his expression unreadable. But he was listening.

Socrates gestured toward the citizens gathered before him. "If I have corrupted the youth, then tell me—what should a teacher do? Should he tell students what to think? Or should he teach them how to think?"

A pause.

Socrates' voice softened. "You fear my questions because they unsettle the foundations of what you believe. But ask yourselves—what is a foundation that cannot withstand a question?"

The room was silent now. Even Antiphon had fallen still.

Alex felt something stir deep within him—a kind of admiration so fierce it almost frightened him.

Socrates stood alone, surrounded by men who feared him, who wanted him gone. And yet, he did not tremble.

He spoke anyway.

The weight of it pressed against Alex's chest.

Could he do that? Could he stand alone, knowing that speaking the truth might cost him everything?

His heart pounded.

For a moment, he almost raised his hand.

To stand with Socrates.

To say something.

But his fingers trembled. His feet felt glued to the floor.

And so, he remained silent.

When Socrates finished, the room did not erupt into cheers or anger. Instead, it was a sea of uncertainty.

Some citizens nodded quietly, their brows furrowed in thought. Others shook their heads, whispering to one another.

"That man speaks madness," one muttered.

"Perhaps…" another murmured. "Or perhaps he speaks wisdom."

Alex turned, searching the faces around him. It was like looking at Athens split in two—one half clinging to tradition, the other half unsure whether Socrates' words had shaken something loose inside them.

He caught sight of Demos again.

His friend stood with the group who disapproved—those who believed Socrates was dangerous.

But he did not look triumphant.

His arms were still crossed. His brow still creased.

As if he, too, was uncertain.

The magistrate banged his staff against the ground, calling the court to order. "The jury will deliberate. The trial will continue tomorrow."

The crowd began to disperse, but the tension lingered in the air.

Alex remained frozen.

He had watched Socrates stand before them all and refuse to bend. He had felt the truth in his words.

And yet…

He had said nothing. His hands curled into fists. He had been too afraid. But tomorrow, the trial would continue. And he would not be silent forever.

6 LEGACY OF QUESTIONS

The courthouse was silent, suffocating beneath the weight of what was about to happen. The entire city of Athens seemed to be holding its breath. The judges, seated high above the gathered crowd, exchanged knowing glances before the eldest among them finally spoke.

"Socrates of Athens," his voice rang out, steady, unwavering, "you have been found guilty of corrupting the youth and disrespecting the gods. The punishment is death."

The words struck like a thunderclap.

Some gasped, others nodded grimly. A handful even cheered, as if a danger had finally been contained.

Alex stood frozen, his mind reeling.

Death?

They were sentencing a man to die because he… asked questions?

He looked at Demos, whose face was tight, unreadable. He saw Thales, eyes downcast, his hands clasped together in quiet sorrow. And then, finally, he looked at Socrates.

The old man stood there, calm as ever. He did not argue, did not beg. He simply smiled, as if he had already made peace with his fate.

"My friends," Socrates said, his voice carrying gently through the hall, "you fear death as if it is the worst thing that can happen to a man. But tell me—what is more dangerous? Death? Or living without truth?"

No one answered.

Alex's hands trembled. He wanted to scream, to protest, to tell them they were wrong. But he couldn't move.

Socrates' eyes flickered to him, and Alex thought, for the briefest moment, that he saw something there— not sadness, not regret, but expectation.

As if Socrates had already placed his legacy in the hands of others.

As if he was waiting for someone else to carry it forward.

Alex swallowed hard.

He wasn't ready. But he had to be.

The Agora was alive with conversation, all centered around the trial. Some debated heatedly, others simply shook their heads, eager to forget.

Alex searched the crowd, spotting Demos and a group of their friends.

They were talking in hushed voices, arguing amongst themselves.

"I told you," Lykos muttered. "Socrates was dangerous. Look what happened."

Demos nodded slowly. "Maybe it's for the best."

Alex stepped forward, his chest burning. "How can you say that?"

Demos turned. "Alex—"

"No!" Alex's voice rose, shaking slightly. "You all listened to him speak. You all heard what he said. Does that sound like a dangerous man to you?"

The group fell silent.

Demos hesitated. "Alex, it's not that simple."

"Yes, it is!" Alex's hands curled into fists. "Socrates didn't hurt anyone. He didn't force anyone to do anything. He only asked us to think."

Some of the boys shifted uncomfortably. Others looked intrigued.

"He taught me that questions aren't dangerous. They're powerful." Alex took a deep breath, his heart pounding. "And if we stop asking them, then maybe we really will be in danger."

For a long moment, no one spoke.

Then, to Alex's surprise, one of the younger boys, Nikos, nodded. "I think he was right."

Another boy murmured in agreement.

Even Demos seemed uncertain.

Alex's voice softened. "You don't have to agree with everything he said. But don't stop thinking. Don't stop asking why."

And for the first time, they listened.

A few days later, Alex sat in the shade of an olive tree near the Agora, a small circle of boys gathered around him. Not everyone had come, but some had. And that was enough.

He took a deep breath.

"All right," he said. "Let's start with a question."

The boys leaned in, listening.

Alex thought for a moment, then smiled.

"What makes a person wise?"

At first, there was silence. Then, slowly, one boy offered, "Knowing a lot of things?"

Another shook his head. "No… I think it's about making good choices."

A third boy frowned. "But how do we know if a choice is good?"

And just like that, a discussion began.

They debated, challenged each other, laughed. Some got frustrated. Others got excited. And for the first time, Alex understood what Socrates must have felt—that moment when a question opened a door in someone's mind, when they discovered something for themselves.

It wasn't just about finding answers.

It was about the journey to seek them.

The sky was painted in gold and pink, the city of Athens stretching before Alex like an unfinished story. He stood on a hillside overlooking the Agora, letting the breeze cool his face.

He imagined Socrates walking these streets, stopping strangers with questions that made them laugh, made them angry, made them think.

Alex had been afraid, once. Afraid to stand alone. Afraid to question too much.

Not anymore.

"I won't stop," he whispered.

He would carry the questions forward. He would challenge his friends, his teachers, maybe even one day the city itself.

Socrates had been one voice.

Now, Alex would be another.

And someday, maybe there would be even more.

As the sun dipped lower, Alex smiled.

The questions had only just begun.

Printed in Great Britain
by Amazon